DATE DUE

DATE DUE

NO	NO	AP 07	AP 27 '06
NO 19 '03	DE 07 '04	AP 18 '05	DE 06 '06
DE 05 '03	DE 09 '04	MY 12 '05	DE 19 '06
DE 08 '03	DE 17 '04	SE 27 '05	JA 31 '07
DE 15 '03	JA 11 '05	DE 2	FE 08 '07
JA 08 '04	JA 19 '05	SE 27 '05	FE 14 '07
JA 20 '04	JA 28 '05	OC 18	FE 26 '07
JA 28 '04	FE 01 '05		AP 19 07
FE 17 '04	FE 11 '05	NO 21 '05	MY 15 '07
MR 18 '04	FE 18 '05	MR 07 '06	OC 09 07

Deer Hunting (The Great Outdoors)

Randy Frahm
AR B.L.: 4.9
Points: 0.5

MG

Deer Hunting

By Randy Frahm

Consultant:
Dr. David M. Knotts
Executive Vice President and CEO
International Hunter Education Association

CAPSTONE
HIGH-INTEREST
BOOKS

an imprint of Capstone Press
Mankato, Minnesota

Capstone High-Interest Books are published by Capstone Press
151 Good Counsel Drive, P.O. Box 669, Mankato, Minnesota 56002
http://www.capstone-press.com

Library of Congress Cataloging-in-Publication Data
Frahm, Randy.
   Deer hunting/by Randy Frahm.
   p. cm.—(The great outdoors)
   Includes bibliographical references and index (p. 48).
   ISBN 0-7368-0912-0
   1. Deer hunting—Juvenile literature. [1. Deer hunting. 2. Hunting.]
I. Title. II. Series.
SK301 .F64 2002
799.2'765—dc21   2001001195

Summary: Describes the equipment, skills, conservation issues, and safety concerns of deer hunting.

Editorial Credits
Carrie A. Braulick, editor; Lois Wallentine, product planning editor; Timothy Halldin,
   cover designer and illustrator; Katy Kudela, photo researcher

Photo Credits
Capstone Press/Gary Sundermeyer, 10 (foreground), 12, 24, 27, 32, 41
Corel, 30 (all), 42 (top, bottom)
Comstock, Inc., 1, 10 (background), 22 (background)
Glenn Hayes/KAC Productions, cover (top right)
Gregg R. Andersen, cover (bottom right), 15, 18, 22 (foreground)
Jeff Henry/Roche Jaune Pictures, Inc., 7, 36, 38, 44
Mark Raycroft, 4, 8, 29, 35
Unicorn Stock Photos/John Ebeling, cover (bottom left); Ted Rose, 21
Visuals Unlimited, 16

2 3 4 5 6 07 06 05 04 03 02

Table of Contents

CHAPTER 1

Deer Hunting

Deer hunting is a popular sport in North America. Deer are the most frequently hunted "big game" animals. These large land animals also include antelope, bears, and buffalo.

History of Deer Hunting

People have hunted deer for thousands of years. American Indians relied on deer meat for food. This meat is called venison. American Indians also made clothes and shelters from deer skins. These skins are called hides. American Indians used deer bones and antlers to make decorations and tools. They even honored deer in special ceremonies. During these events, American Indians recognized the importance of deer in their lives.

Early North American settlers also depended on deer. They ate venison and made clothing from

People sometimes use bows to hunt deer.

deer hides. Settlers often sold or traded venison to stores. They also traded deer hides for items in stores. Some settlers even used deer hides to pay taxes to the government.

Deer Hunting Today

Today, North Americans continue to hunt deer. People hunt deer for many reasons. Many hunters eat venison from the deer they kill. They may make ground venison or venison steaks. Deer hunters also hunt to spend time outdoors. Hunters can observe a variety of plant and animal life. Some deer hunters enjoy spending time with friends or family members as they hunt.

Other hunters enjoy hunting for a "trophy" deer. A trophy deer is a male deer with very large or unusually shaped antlers. Hunters may display the mounted head of a trophy deer in their homes. People who mount animals are called taxidermists. They treat the skin of dead animals with chemicals. They often create a clay model of an animal's parts to preserve its

Deer hunters sometimes hunt with others.

structure. These activities make the mounted models appear lifelike.

North American Deer

All deer share some features. Deer have narrow heads, large ears, short tails, and hooves. All deer have good senses of smell and hearing. Deer are herbivores. They eat only plants. Deer eat grasses, leaves, nuts, and fruits. They also depend on farm crops such as corn and wheat for food.

People can hunt for mule deer in western North America.

Five deer species live in North America. All animals within a species share certain physical features. North American deer species include white-tailed deer, mule deer, elk, moose, and caribou.

White-Tailed and Mule Deer

White-tailed deer and mule deer are the most common North American deer species. These deer are hunted more often than other North

American species. Hunters use similar techniques to hunt white-tailed and mule deer.

Male white-tailed and mule deer are called bucks. Females are called does. Only bucks grow antlers. The antlers fall off each winter. Bucks grow new sets of antlers during late spring and throughout the summer.

White-tailed deer live within a large area of North America. This area is called their range. The white-tailed deer's range extends from southern Canada to the southern United States. White-tailed deer are most common in the eastern half of North America.

White-tailed deer can adapt to various habitats. These natural conditions and places in which deer live include forests, swamps, fields, and prairies. White-tailed deer also live in cities.

Mule deer live in western North America. Their range extends south from the western Canadian provinces and territories of Yukon, British Columbia, Alberta, and Saskatchewan to western Texas. It then extends west to the Pacific coast. Mule deer have habitats in hilly and mountainous areas. They also live in deserts, meadows, forests, prairies, and fields.

Venison Meatballs

Ingredients:

2 eggs
1/3 cup (75 mL) milk
2/3 cup (150 mL) bread crumbs
2/3 cup (150 mL) Parmesan
  cheese
2 teaspoons (10 mL) dried parsley
1 1/2 teaspoons (7 mL) garlic
  powder
Salt and pepper

1 pound (455 grams) ground
  venison
1 28-ounce (840-gram) can
  or jar of spaghetti sauce
Cooked pasta

Equipment:

Large bowl
Spoon, egg beater,
  or automatic mixer
Mixing spoon
Large frying pan with cover

1. Combine eggs with milk in a large bowl. Mix with spoon, egg beater, or mixer.

2. Add bread crumbs, Parmesan cheese, parsley, garlic powder, and salt and pepper to egg and milk mixture. Mix these ingredients with a mixing spoon.

3. Add venison. Knead all of the ingredients with your hands until well blended. Form into meatballs about the size of golf balls.

4. Brown the meatballs on all sides in frying pan over medium heat. Add spaghetti sauce.

5. Cover pan and simmer for 1 hour over low heat.

6. Serve on top of cooked pasta.

Children should have adult supervision.

The Rut

The mating season for white-tailed and mule deer is called the rut. The rut occurs each fall. In northern areas, the rut usually begins in late October or early November. In southern areas of the United States, the rut usually begins in middle to late November. The rut usually lasts about three months.

The rut's season can vary depending on the weather. Cool weather early in the season can cause the rut to start sooner. Hot weather may delay the rut.

Deer hunting seasons occur during the rut. People are allowed to hunt during these periods in the fall. Deer often travel to look for mates during the rut. This activity makes them easier to hunt. Deer hide more often during other seasons to protect themselves from predators. These animals hunt other animals for food.

CHAPTER 2

Equipment

Modern deer hunters use a variety of equipment. They use guns or bows and arrows to kill deer. Hunters also use equipment to stay safe and comfortable.

Rifles

Hunters can use a variety of guns to shoot deer. Most deer hunters use rifles. A rifle shoots bullets. A metal case called a cartridge holds each bullet. The cartridge has powder that creates an explosive charge. When a hunter shoots, the charge pushes the bullet out of a long metal tube called the barrel. The barrel is located at the front of a gun. Deer hunters who use rifles often can hit targets at least 100 yards (91 meters) away.

Rifles can have five different actions. A rifle's action loads, fires, and ejects cartridges. Actions include pump, bolt, break, lever, and

Many deer hunters use rifles.

semi-automatic. Hunters must operate bolt-, break-, pump-, and lever-action rifles by hand. They load a new cartridge into these rifles after they shoot. Rifles with semi-automatic actions eject and load cartridges automatically after hunters shoot.

Rifles come in different calibers. Caliber is the measurement of the circular barrel's diameter. Diameter is the distance from one side of a circle to the other. Caliber often is measured in thousandths of an inch. It also can be measured in millimeters.

Calibers can range from about .17 to .458. Most deer hunters choose rifles that are .30 caliber or larger. Rifles that are .30 caliber have a barrel diameter of about 7.5 millimeters (.3 inch). Rifles with high calibers have more power than rifles with low calibers.

Rifles often have a scope attached to them. This viewing instrument makes the target's image appear closer. A scope helps hunters aim.

It is illegal for hunters to use rifles in some locations. These areas often have many people living nearby. The areas also may have few trees

Rifle

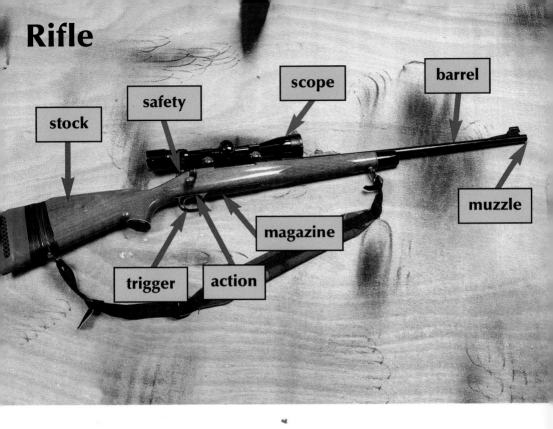

stock · safety · scope · barrel · muzzle · magazine · trigger · action

to block a bullet. A bullet can travel more than
1 mile (1.6 kilometers) and hit a person in
these places.

Shotguns

Some deer hunters use shotguns. Shotguns can
fire pellets made of lead or steel. These pellets
are called shot. Shotguns also can fire a single
piece of lead called a slug. Most deer hunters
use slugs. A case called a shell holds the pellets
or slug. Shells usually are made of plastic.

Deer hunters load shells made of plastic into their shotguns.

Shotguns have different gauges. The number of lead balls that fit inside a shotgun's bore determines its gauge. The bore is the barrel's inside diameter. Together, the lead balls weigh 1 pound (.5 kilogram). For example, a 12-gauge shotgun fits 12 lead balls with a combined weight of 1 pound inside its bore.

Shotgun gauges range from .410 to 10. The .410 is the smallest gauge. Gauges that are between .410 and 10 from smallest to largest are the 28-gauge, 20-gauge, 16-gauge, and 12-gauge shotguns. The .410 is the only gauge that is measured in inches. Other shotgun gauges are measured in millimeters. Most deer hunters use 12-, 16- or 20-gauge shotguns.

Guns with smaller gauge numbers are more powerful than guns with higher gauge numbers. For example, a 12-gauge shotgun is more powerful than a 20-gauge shotgun.

Hunters consider their distance from a deer before they shoot. Hunters can use shotguns to shoot deer within a distance of about 100 yards (91 meters).

Some hunters who use slugs attach scopes to their shotguns. The scopes help hunters shoot at distant targets.

Muzzleloaders

Some deer hunters use muzzleloaders. Early North American settlers used these guns to shoot deer. Many hunters who use muzzleloaders enjoy the challenge of shooting deer with these guns. Deer hunters use muzzleloaders that fire round lead balls or cone-shaped pieces of lead. Many hunters use .45 caliber muzzleloaders. But some

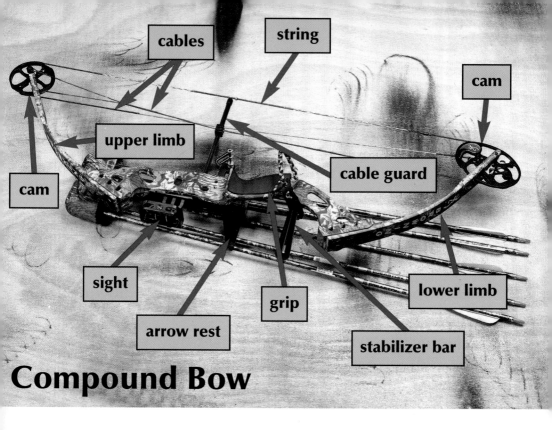

cables

string

cam

cam

upper limb

cable guard

sight

lower limb

grip

arrow rest

stabilizer bar

Compound Bow

deer hunters use muzzleloaders with a caliber of
.50 or more.

Hunters need to reload muzzleloaders by
hand after shooting the gun. This feature makes
muzzleloaders slower to use than most rifles.
Hunters place the piece of lead into the muzzle
with gun powder. The muzzle is located at the
end of a gun's barrel. The powder creates an
explosive charge when the gun is fired. Hunters
can shoot at deer up to about 100 yards
(91 meters) away with muzzleloaders.

Bowhunting Equipment

People who bowhunt use a bow to shoot arrows at deer. Bowhunters place an arrow against a bow's string. They pull the string back and let it go. The string then snaps forward and causes the arrow to move toward its target.

Many hunters use modern compound bows. These bows reduce the amount of force needed to hold the string back. Compound bows sometimes are made of fiberglass. This strong, lightweight material is made of woven glass fibers. Bows also can be made of lightweight metal.

Arrows are made of strong, lightweight materials. They may be made of a soft material called graphite. They also may be made of a metal called aluminum.

Arrows usually have sharp points made of steel at one end and feathers at the other end. The feathers are made of synthetic fabrics. These fabrics are made by people. The feathers help keep the arrows on course as they travel.

Bowhunters must be closer to their target than hunters with guns. Most bowhunters shoot at deer less than 50 yards (46 meters) away from them.

Many hunters believe bowhunting is more difficult than hunting with guns for this reason.

Bowhunters must be accurate. They need to hit a deer in the lungs, liver, or heart. A deer hit in these vital organs usually dies quickly from blood loss. Deer hit in other body areas may not die. They can suffer from serious injuries.

Clothing

Deer hunters should dress properly. Their clothing should keep them warm in cold weather. Hunters often wear several layers of clothing. They can add and remove layers to keep themselves comfortable. The outside layer of clothing sometimes is made of nylon. This strong material is wind- and water-resistant. Deer hunters should wear heavy coats, hats, gloves, and boots in cold weather.

Hunters' clothing should help them remain unnoticed by deer as they hunt. Hunters should wear soft clothing to prevent noise. Deer that hear unfamiliar noises may run away or move to hidden areas. Deer hunters also may wash their hunting clothes in special soap that removes odors. Deer may avoid places where they smell unfamiliar scents.

Bowhunters should wear camouflage clothing.

Bowhunters should wear camouflage clothing. This clothing blends into the surroundings. It helps hunters hide from deer.

Hunters who use guns should wear brightly-colored clothing. Many states and provinces require these hunters to wear blaze orange or red. These colors help hunters see each other. The colors can prevent hunters from mistaking a person for a deer.

Hunters with guns and bowhunters usually hunt during different times to help protect hunters

Equipment

- Rifle, shotgun, or muzzleloader
- Bow and arrows
- Bullets
- Shells
- Lead balls for muzzleloader
- Sharp knife
- Calls
- Deodorants for scent
- First aid kit
- Scents to attract deer
- Binoculars
- Compass

from injury. Hunters with guns may not see bowhunters hunting at the same time.

Other Equipment

Deer hunters carry other equipment. They may carry this equipment in a backpack. Hunters should bring binoculars. This viewing instrument allows hunters to see deer from a distance. Some hunters bring a compass. A flashlight can be useful to hunters if it becomes dark before they return home. Deer hunters may use special deodorants to hide their scent.

Hunters should bring a first aid kit. These kits contain items such as gauze, medicine tape, and adhesive bandages. Hunters can use the contents of a first aid kit in case of accidents or injuries.

Hunters should have a sharp knife to field dress a deer. They cut out areas of the deer's body such as the lungs and stomach after they kill it. These parts can spoil the meat if they remain in the deer.

Some deer hunters use calls. These objects make deer sounds when hunters use them. The calls sound similar to the noises deer make to attract each other during the rut. Deer sometimes approach the areas where hunters use calls.

CHAPTER 3

Skills and Techniques

Hunters use various methods to hunt deer. Some hunters walk around to look for deer or walk toward deer that they see. Hunters also may wait for deer to come near them. They often use scents and calls to attract deer. They may use a lotion or spray that smells like a doe to attract bucks. Hunters also may use a call that sounds like a buck to attract does.

Deer hunters should know what times of day to find deer. White-tailed and mule deer usually eat around sunrise and before sunset. They move during periods of low light to avoid being seen by predators.

Some hunters look for deer with binoculars before they approach them.

Scouting

Deer hunters should scout an area before they hunt. Deer hunters decide where they want to hunt when they scout. They then learn about the area. They find out what types of deer live nearby. They may look for rubs. These scratches on tree trunks are left by bucks. Bucks grind their antlers against trees during the rut. Many people believe bucks leave rubs to mark their territories.

Hunters also look for deer tracks. White-tailed and mule deer tracks are about 2.5 to 3.5 inches (6.4 to 8.9 centimeters) long. Buck tracks usually are slightly larger than doe tracks.

Hunters may look for deer droppings. These droppings are small and oval. They usually are in piles. Each dropping is about .75 inch (1.9 centimeters) long.

Hunters look for other deer signs. They look for trails that deer regularly use. Deer often follow the same paths to and from their feeding areas. Deer trails often are between small clearings and woods. Hunters also may try to

Bucks often make rubs with their antlers.

discover where deer rest. They look for areas where grass or weeds are pressed to the ground.

Stand Hunting

Hunters may place platforms in trees after they have scouted an area. These platforms are called stands. They usually are about 10 to 15 feet (3 to 4.6 meters) above the ground. Hunters use stands so deer cannot easily see or smell them. Deer have difficulty smelling objects above them. Hunters wait in their stands for deer to come by. They often place stands near deer trails and deer feeding areas.

Hunters must remove stands that are on public land after the hunting season. Some hunters build permanent stands on private land.

Some stands are portable. Hunters can easily move these stands to different areas.

Blind Hunting

Many hunters use natural features such as hills, trees, and weeds to hide from deer. Other hunters hide from deer in blinds. Hunters place or build these hidden shelters on the ground. Some hunters purchase blinds made of camouflage

Some blinds are made of camouflage cloth.

cloth from stores. Other hunters create their own blinds. Hunters often place their blinds near deer trails and feeding areas.

Hunters can build blinds in various ways. They may place large branches around themselves. Deer hunters also can attach grasses and leaves to netting. They may attach cornstalks together and stand them up. The hunters then can hide behind them.

Deer Vital Areas

Stalking

Hunters who stalk move around often. They hope to see a deer as they travel. Hunters who stalk usually hunt alone. They walk very slowly into the wind. The wind then blows their scent away from their path. They often stop and move their head from side to side to look for deer. Hunters who stalk try to hide behind trees, ridges, or other structures.

Hunters often stalk during times of high winds or wet weather. High winds produce noise that can cover the sounds of hunters. Rain and snow help make leaves and grasses less likely to snap and crunch under hunters' feet.

CHAPTER 4

Conservation

Deer are one of the most common North American animals. Scientists estimate that the U.S. deer population is between 25 million and 30 million. But hunters still need to keep conservation in mind. They should follow state and provincial hunting regulations to help protect deer populations.

Deer Population Problems

Too few or too many deer can change an area's ecosystem. This system is the relationship between animals and their environment. Today, many areas throughout North America have large deer populations. The deer often eat farmers' crops. They also may cause traffic accidents.

Deer in areas with large deer populations are more likely to die than deer in less populated

Deer hunters must know state or provincial hunting regulations.

areas. Many of these deer are unable to find food during winter. The deer then become weak. Weak deer are more likely to get diseases. The diseases often spread quickly in areas with large deer populations. The deer are more likely to come in contact with each other than in less populated areas.

Too few deer also can change an area's ecosystem. Deer predators may be less able to find food. These animals then may become sick or die.

Regulations

State and provincial agencies set various regulations. They examine the number of deer in certain areas. They then base their regulations on these numbers.

The limit is the number of deer a hunter is allowed to kill throughout the season. Many North American hunters can only kill one deer per season. But other hunters can kill more than two deer per season.

The length of deer hunting seasons varies according to the equipment hunters use. Many

Deer hunters with guns usually hunt at different times than bowhunters.

rifle and shotgun seasons begin in late October and last until mid-November. Bowhunting season can begin in early September and last through December or January. But bowhunters and hunters with guns usually do not hunt at the same time. Hunters who use muzzleloaders also have separate seasons from hunters who use rifles or shotguns.

Deer hunters must fill out a tag after they kill a deer.

State and provincial agencies set other regulations. Hunters need to purchase licenses to deer hunt. They need to put tags on their deer after they kill them. Deer hunters receive the tags when they purchase licenses. They mark the date they killed the deer on the tag. They also mark the location of where the deer was killed.

People often must be at least 12 years old to deer hunt. These hunters often need to complete a hunter education course. This course teaches people how to safely handle guns and bowhunting equipment. It also teaches people how to identify animals before they shoot and how to handle emergencies. All state and provincial wildlife agencies offer hunter education courses.

State and provincial regulations change from year to year. Hunters must learn about the changes before each hunting season.

CHAPTER 5

Safety

Deer hunters should follow safety guidelines. Hunters should keep track of the weather conditions. A snow storm can cause hunters to become lost. Hunters may have difficulty seeing during heavy snowfall.

Gun Safety

Deer hunters who use guns should follow certain guidelines. Deer hunters should let other hunters know their location. They also should avoid shooting where other hunters are located. They should store guns unloaded. They should avoid jumping or climbing with a loaded gun. Deer hunters need to identify their target before they shoot. They should never point their gun at another person. Hunters

Deer hunters should stay aware of the weather conditions and their surroundings as they hunt.

should keep their finger off the trigger except when firing.

Deer hunters must make sure to keep the safety on until they are ready to shoot. This device prevents hunters from accidentally firing a gun.

Other Safety Concerns

Hunters should follow other safety guidelines. They should learn the weather forecast and dress properly. They should know how to use the items in their first aid kit. Safe hunters also learn about the wildlife and plants in their hunting areas. They do not bother other wildlife. They learn about harmful plants such as poison ivy. This plant can cause a skin rash.

Hunters should wear a fall-restraint device when they are in a tree stand. These harnesses strap safely around a hunter's waist and shoulders. The safety harnesses hold hunters in case of a fall.

Deer hunters should make sure they know each other's hunting locations.

Safe hunters always tell someone where they will be hunting. Others can then search for hunters who do not return at the expected time.

Safe deer hunters are prepared for their adventure. They try to prevent injuries and accidents. These deer hunters help make their activity safer for themselves and others.

North American deer species include white-tailed deer, mule deer, elk, moose, and caribou. White-tailed deer and mule deer are the most common of these deer species.

White-Tailed Deer

White-tailed deer live throughout the United States except in some southwestern states such as Nevada and Utah. White-tailed deer also live in southern Canada.

Description: White-tailed deer usually are brown to red-brown. Their coats often turn gray-brown during winter. White-tailed deer have a white patch on their throat, nose, and around their eyes. The underside of their tails is white. Male white-tails usually weigh between 75 and 300 pounds (34 and 136 kilograms). Females usually weigh between 50 and 200 pounds (23 and 91 kilograms).

Habitat: deserts, forests, marshes, prairies, fields

Food: grasses, shrubs, buds, leaves, acorns, berries, corn, apples, alfalfa, tree bark, twigs

Mule Deer

Mule deer live only in the western parts of North America. They live in areas west of Iowa, Missouri, Arkansas, and Louisiana.

Description: Mule deer are gray-brown. Their tails are white with a black tip. Their ears have black edges. They often have a white patch on their throat and chin. The white may extend to a mule deer's nose and face. Males usually weigh between 125 and 400 pounds (57 and 181 kilograms). Females usually weigh between 100 and 200 pounds (45 and 91 kilograms).

Habitat: mountains, deserts, prairies, forests, valleys, fields

Food: grasses, shrubs, buds, leaves, fruit, wheat, alfalfa

Words to Know

barrel (BA-ruhl)—the long, tube-shaped metal part of a gun; bullets or pellets travel through a gun's barrel.

blind (BLINDE)—a hidden place from which deer hunters can shoot deer

caliber (CAH-luh-bur)—the diameter of a gun's barrel

habitat (HAB-uh-tat)—the places and natural conditions in which an animal lives

hide (HYDE)—a deer's skin

limit (LIM-it)—the number of deer that a hunter can kill in one season

rub (RUB)—the tree marking a buck makes with its antlers

safety (SAYF-tee)—a device that prevents a gun from firing

shot (SHOT)—lead or steel pellets in a shell

To Learn More

Bair, Diane, and Pamela Wright. *Deer Watching.* Wildlife Watching. Mankato, Minn.: Capstone Books, 2000.

Ceaser, Jonathan. *Essential Deer Hunting for Teens.* Outdoor Life. New York: Rosen Publishing Group, 2000.

Sneath, Jerry E. *Aim of the Hunt.* Bellwood, Penn.: Catlett Publishing, 1996.

Useful Addresses

Canadian Wildlife Service
Environment Canada
Ottawa, ON K1A 0H3
Canada

International Hunter Education Association
P.O. Box 490
Wellington, CO 80549

Mule Deer Foundation
1005 Terminal Way, Suite 170
Reno, NV 89502

Quality Deer Management Association
P.O. Box 227
Watkinsville, GA 30677

U.S. Fish and Wildlife Service
4401 North Fairfax Drive
Arlington, VA 22203

Internet Sites

Canadian Wildlife Service
http://www.cws-scf.ec.gc.ca/cwshom_e.html

International Hunter Education Association
http://www.ihea.com

National Bowhunter Education Foundation
http://www.nbef.org

U.S. Fish and Wildlife Service
http://www.fws.gov

Index